GOETIC LITURGY

HADEAN

GOETIC LITURGY
Copyright © 2015 Jake Stratton Kent
Published by Hadean Press, France.
www.hadeanpress.com
'Female Confession' by William Behun.

This text first appeared in *The Equinox: British Journal of Thelema*, issues 9, 10, and 11, as 'Liturgical Approaches to Invocation & Evocation', parts I, II, and III.

ISBN 978 1 907881 43 5

Jake Stratton-Kent has asserted his moral right to be identified as the author of this work.

GOETIC LITURGY

JAKE STRATTON-KENT

TABLE OF CONTENTS

PART I

Invocation & Evocation

The purpose of this book is to make available a process of ceremonial composition of use in the invocation of deities and the evocation of spirits. The underlying conception involves extending and building upon a core ritual of the Thelemic liturgy. The principal ritual, encompassing the whole process, is the rite known as *Pyramidos*; an extremely versatile and potent ceremonial frame. *Pyramidos* in its essential form is an initiation ritual in several parts; some of which can be detached for other purposes, particularly invocation. It is chiefly this capacity of *Pyramidos* that will be discussed. Included in this three part text will be:

The original sub-rituals of Opening and Closing from Pyramidos;

Two variant forms of the above;

Invocations integrated with the underlying cosmology;

Sub-rituals appropriate to Invocations and Conjurations; designed to facilitate various adaptation

For evocations the spirit hierarchies most compatible with the conception and cosmology of the rite are: the spirits of the *True Grimoire*, of the Graeco-Egyptian papyri, and of Archaic Goetia.

In addition there will rubrics and commentaries making plain what is involved in the various procedures. This material is from *The Equinox: British Journal of Thelema*, issues 9, 10, and 11, published by Hadean Press.

The approach underlying this paper is a well tested, fully integrated ritual methodology; it lends itself to composition of additional invocations and adaptation by individual magicians. The method is made clear not by dry and doctrinaire description but by example, as well as the inclusion of commentary and alternative rubrics.

A few words of introduction and explanation are called for, even for those who may be familiar with *Liber Pyramidos*. The original rite consisted of various sub-rituals which could be used together or independently, of which the most important for general purposes were the Opening and Closing. The ritual could be performed solo or by two magicians, and is closely related to another ritual, known as TROA, in which these two magicians were officers in a ritual of initiation; this presupposes an additional person be present, a Candidate for initiation. *Pyramidos* on the other hand was essentially a ritual of self initiation, the components of which could also be used in rites of invocation and evocation. Examples of this latter use may be found in *Grimorium Sanctissimum*; the record of the *Paris Working*, and elsewhere.

Further analysis of this ritual in various forms will follow in parts II and III of this book. For the time being it is necessary to say that in the original rite the principles of Life and Death, or two godforms, Asi and Hoor-Apep, were represented by two magicians or united in one. These two were theoretically stationed at the two base points of a triangle, and the Eastern focus at the apex represented the united polarities, represented by the twin serpents of the caduceus of Tahuti. For convenience this latter principle can be termed 'Wisdom'. In the variant rituals however East is no longer the nominal focus, but the other two points thus:

South West in which the two officers are Death and Wisdom, Hoor-Apep and Tahuti, invoking Life or Asi.

North West, in which the two officers are Life and Wisdom, Asi and Tahuti invoking Death or Hoor-Apep.

Close examination of the ritual known as *Liber Israfel* or *Majesty of Godhead* shows that this invocation was either composed, or adapted, to be framed within the Opening and Closing of the Pyramid. In one of the rites given later this precedent has been followed, substituting an invocation of Heka or Hecate. This invocation could equally be substituted by the Invocation of Isis, which follows after this introduction. The wand mentioned in the text is equally useful for any form of this ritual, and should either bear or be understood to include a serpent or serpents on its shaft, and an eight spoked 'Wheel of the Spirit' at the tip.

It is highly recommended that the analysis of *Liber Israfel* in Crowley's *Magick* be closely examined in putting any of these rituals into operation. It is then a fairly simple matter to put in place adaptations by which evocations can be very readily performed. Additionally the diagram of the Circle in *Magick* has close connections with *Pyramidos*, as do the various plates in *Treasure House of Images*. Comprehension of these points will show very clearly that a thirteen-fold structure is involved in all of them, a fact which has potent implications for the use of the English Alphabet of 26 letters in Thelemic qaballa.

Further, the structure and hierarchy of the *True Grimoire* has certain affinities with the structure of *Pyramidos* and its godforms. Adaptations of Pyramidos to rites of evocation are described following upon these affinities.

Finally, certain sadomasochistic elements have been removed from *Pyramidos* for this publication, for the simple reason the liturgist responsible does not find them necessary. In their place a simple psycho-physical shock has been evolved from the existing employment of water in the ritual. This usage derives from the writings of Lucius Apuleius, and consists of using water from a wide vessel to douse the top of the head. Sufficient water should be used, either by cupping two hands or immersing the head, that a definite physiological shock results. Alternatively, or in addition, those who are so inclined may reintroduce the original use of a ritual knife.

AN INVOCATION OF ISIS

The original inspiration for this ritual was twofold. The first was of course *Liber Israfel*, and the enlightening commentary on this ritual in *Book 4*. The second is the account of Crowley's abandoned intention to completely revise the G.˙.D.˙. rites on Thelemic lines as detailed in Francis King's *Ritual Magic in England*, chapter 13, in particular the line 'the Invocations are to be got from the Egyptian papyri as taught...', plainly implying that Israfel rather than being simply a one-off was an example of a genre magicians could implement themselves. Our performance of the above ritual differs to a degree from Israfel as described by Crowley in *Book 4*, and in particular in the fourth section. But this and other matters are best left to the students 'right ingeniuum'. It is enough for me that the ritual, and the idea of its construction, is now made available to a wider audience. The various parties who have performed it in the past have all declared themselves impressed with the results, but that is another story. Feedback is appreciated and answered, c/o the publishers.

The ritual itself may be inserted between the Opening and Closing of the Pyramid, either the conventional form or the SW variant which appears at the end of this article. An alternative rubric detailing other options is appended at the conclusion of the ritual.

The Invocation of Isis

I

I invoke Isis, the Lady of Life and Love, the Goddess of Mystery and Truth!

(If desired make Invoking Hexagram(s) as appropriate with A.M.E.N. Names or other Great Name. Alternatively declare the Names in the quarters without hexagrams)

O Thou Continuous One of Heaven, Queen of Infinite Space & the Infinite Stars thereof – the Night Sky's Queen! Thee, Thee, I invoke!

Thou Who art crowned with the Moon's Disk, on Whose brow is the Serpent of Wisdom! Thee, Thee I invoke!

Thou who wieldest the Lotus Wand! Thee, Thee I invoke!

Thou who bearest in Thy left hand the Rose & Cross of Light & Life: Thee, Thee I invoke!

Thou Whose skin is of finest gold, for Thou art clothed with the Sun! Thee, Thee I invoke!

Thou Sister & Bride of Osiris the Slain One; Who bore Horus in Her Womb, fleeing the Blasting Winds of Typhon! Thee, Thee I invoke!

Thou Whose Headdress is of gleaming white, whose Robe glows as the azure sky! Thee, Thee I invoke!

Thou Knower of the Name of Ra! Mistress of Magick & Mystery, Thee, Thee I invoke!

Thou Who gathered the limbs of wronged Osiris, Who didst beget Horus upon His body! Thee, Thee I invoke!

Thou, the Nourisher of the Conquering Child, the infant Har-Par-Kraatist: Thee, Thee I invoke!

II

(Assume God-form of Isis)

Behold I am ever present – for I am the Universal Mother who hearest every prayer.

I am Nature, Queen of all the Elements, Primordial Child of Time – the Sovereign of all things!

I am the Queen of the Dead & of the Company of the Gods!

In Myself I encompass all the Company of Heaven!

I open the Gates of Death & of Life, Mother of the Midnight Sun!

I am seated in the Boat of Ra in its journey through the Underworld; by my Gate does it mount unto Heaven!

Behold! She is in me & I in Her!

I am She, Goddess of the Beginning – the Mother of the Sun:

Knower of the Courses of Heaven, Knower of Light and Darkness;

For I am Nuit the Mother of the Gods,

I am Serqet the Scorpion in the Wilderness,

I am Maut, Vulture Guardian of the Realm of Egypt.

Mine are the Mighty Words of Enchantment, and Mine the Wisdom of the pure in heart!

My tongue is the sanctuary of Maat, Goddess of Truth!

For I have framed speech for My mouth and the mantras of the Nations are the echoes of My Name!

My Will is accomplished by Day and by Night,

The Desire of My Heart realises itself, coming forth as the Children of Nu in the Days of Becoming.

I am Eternal, therefore all things are My designs, therefore do all things obey my word!

III

Therefore do Thou come forth unto me from Thine Abode in the Silence: Supernal Wisdom! All Light! All Love!

AST! INANNA! SOPHIA! MRI – O – DOM!

By whatsoever Name Thou art called by all the Nations of

the Earth, Thou art Nameless unto Eternity: Come Thou
forth I say and aid and guard me in this Work of Art.

Thou that risest with the Dog-Star, Herald of the Life
Giving Waters!

Thou Queen alike of Heaven and of Hell!

Thou Mistress of the Light and of the Darkness!

Clothed with the Sun and Crowned with Celestial Stars!

Come Thou forth I say, Come Thou forth! And make
all spirits subject unto me, so that every spirit of the
Firmament and of the Aethyr, on dry land and in the
Water, upon the Earth or under the Earth, of Whirling
Air or of Rushing Fire, and every Spell and Scourge of
God the Vast One may be obedient unto me!

OMARI TESSALA MARAX
TESSALA DODI PHORNEPAX
AMRI RADARA POLIAX
ARMANA PILIU.

AMRI RADARA PILIU SON
MARI NARYA BARBITON
MADARA ANAPHAX SARPEDON
ANDALA HRILIU!

I make open the Gate of Bliss,
I descend from the Palace of the Stars;
I overshadow you with My Wings
Ye Children of Earth that are gathered in the Hall of
Truth!

Above, the gemmed azure is
The naked splendour of Nuit;
She bends in ecstasy to kiss
The secret ardours of Hadit.
The winged globe, the starry blue,
Are mine, o Ankh-af-na-Khonsu!

*(Make the 'Qabalistic Cross' and fold the arms on breast as
follows):*

(Raising hand above head and lowering it to forehead, say):
O Glory be...
(Lowering hand to groin, say):
 unto Thee...
*(Retrace a line to the centre of the chest then touching the right
and left shoulder in turn, say):*
Through all Time and through all Space,
Touching the centre of this Cross of Light, say again
Glory...
*(Folding the arms one over the other in the position of Osiris
Risen, say as the right hand rests on the left shoulder):*
and Glory...
(and as the left crosses it and rests on the right shoulder):
upon Glory Everlastingly...
(Resting in this position conclude):
AMEN, & AMEN & AMEN.
*(Conclude with the Sign of Silence, imagining the godform to be
of vast size and feeling the footstep of the god shaking the earth
as you advance your foot).*

*(Here may be inserted the sacrament, followed by AL I.vs.61,
read by the Priestess).*

The Ending of the Words is the Word ABRAHADABRA!

ALTERNATIVE RUBRIC

The Ritual has been presented without accompanying 'stage directions', firstly to protect certain formulae (possibly unimportant in themselves save to those using them, others may of course devise their own), and secondly because the ritual is fairly versatile, and one set of stage directions would only suit one purpose. If the *Pyramidos* Opening and Closing are not used it is recommended that the Opening Ceremony takes some such form as this following:

'Let the Rituals be rightly performed with Joy & Beauty!'

Banishing Ritual with Names Fiat, Apep, Babalon, Aiwaz.

Purifications with Water with words 'For pure will, unassuaged of purpose, delivered from the lust of result, is every way perfect' and a triple elevation of the cup with the words 'Azure.. Lidded... Woman...'

Consecrations with Fire with the words 'I am uplifted in thine heart and the kisses of the stars rain hard upon thy body' and again a triple elevation of the censer and the words 'Azure.. Lidded... Woman...'

The Invoking Ritual of the AL Sigil or Pentagram with the names Christ (or Khephra), Typhon, Jesus, Hoor-Ra.

Then a Reading of Chapter II of LXV (plus Statement of Intent/Oath if and as required). The Invocation should then be preceded by another potent and formal ritual, for instance the Headless Rite.

The various stages of the Opening and of the Main Ritual allow for different personnel as appropriate, but occult principles should be adhered to in the allocation, rather than some idea of fairness with no regard for the work undertaken. As for stage directions, 'Aid and guard me in this work of art' is an appropriate point for talismanic work to be completed, with the formation of the magical link in the case of possession states. The Ecstatic Paean which opens part four should be recited as a poem, not vibrated as single words, rhythm and metre not bellowings! At this point, the priestess(es) may prepare the sacrament with the words (softly spoken) SE GU MELAI. Finally, the 'Glory Be Unto Thee...' section is of course the Qaballistic Cross as used in *Liber 963* and elsewhere, it should be performed by all present if possible.

Occasions on which this rite may be performed (and thus the selection of the appropriate Invoking Hexagrams) comprise a wide selection. Lunar and Venusian occasions suggest themselves: Isis as Queen of Night is readily accommodated into the Witchcraft; a Sun-Venus rite would not be inappropriate; Via Combusta can be really excellent if properly understood and applied, with attention to 'stage directions' a priority; similar considerations apply to Moon Void of Course.

RITUALS OF EVOCATION

The ritual which follows is devised as an invocation of a deity with the specific purpose of evoking spirits by the authority of the deity concerned. Since this differs from Invocation pure and simple additional sub-rituals are required, within the same general framework. The basic pattern involved is Opening, Oath and Confession, Invocation, Evocation and Conversation of the hierarchy of spirits over which the deity invoked has authority, and finally the Closing. As each level of the hierarchy is evoked they are greeted accordingly, and conversed with, the 'License to depart' may then given to each in turn, before moving on to the next level of the hierarchy. The License will often be omitted until a later stage if the spirits are to be welcomed to participate in the sacrament, and then it is performed after that stage of the Closing ritual. The 'License' of the spirits is not an exorcism or banishing as often understood. The spirit may be invited to return to a habitual consecrated image or prepared vessel, or a predetermined place. The Opening and Closing rituals for the deities and spirits concerned in this first part of this book are given at the end.

THE OATH AND CONFESSION

Singular form:

I N, (an initiate of the Order NN) am come to this Working of Magick Art: To conjure the Spirits of the Aeons named N and N... That my Will which is..... may be accomplished; that in working my will I may increase my knowledge, wisdom and power. That in so doing I may come to the accomplishment of the Great Work. In the Names of Nuit, Hadit and Ra Hoor Khut; So Mote it Be. ✠AMEN✠.

Plural form:

We N and N and N, (initiates of the Order NN) are come to this Working of Magick Art: To conjure the Spirits of the Aeons named N and N... That our Will which is..... may be accomplished; that in working our will we may increase our knowledge, wisdom and power. That in so doing we may come to the accomplishment of the Great Work. In the Names of Nuit, Hadit and Ra Hoor Khut. So Mote it Be. ✠AMEN✠.

As is likely clear enough, the phrase in brackets may be omitted if the ritual is performed by a magician uninvolved in magical orders, or if the ritual is 'unofficial', etc. The names of spirits it is proposed to evoke are said where N and N occurs; Astaroth, the Chief of the spirits; her deputy Nebiros and then any or all of his subordinates. The purpose for which the ceremony is performed is then stated. The three deity names at the conclusion of the Oath may be replaced if desired with the names of the Three Chiefs of Spirits or the three deity forms of the Pyramidos rite, although these may be taken as implied.

The Oath and Confession are essentially one. Therefore, immediately the Oath is completed kneel and bow before the Altar to make the Confession. This should be performed in utmost humility and ecstatic surrender. With your head down raise up the wands one after the other, and confess; raising the wand of evocation (right hand) for each accusation, and that of divination (left hand) for each 'I am under the Shadow of the Wings':

THE CONFESSION

Male form:

Yea! But I am a fool, a flutterer!
I am under the Shadow of the Wings!
I am a liar and a sorcerer.
I am under the Shadow of the Wings!
I am so fickle that I scorn the bridle.
I am under the Shadow of the Wings!
I am unchaste, voluptuous and idle.
I am under the Shadow of the Wings!
I am a bully and a tyrant crass.
I am under the Shadow of the Wings!

I am as dense and as stubborn as an ass.
I am under the Shadow of the Wings!
I am untrusty, cruel and insane.
I am under the Shadow of the Wings!
I am a fool and frivolous and vain.
I am under the Shadow of the Wings!
I am a weakling and a coward; I cringe.
I am under the Shadow of the Wings!
I am a catamite and cunnilinge.
I am under the Shadow of the Wings!
I am a glutton, a besotted wight.
I am under the Shadow of the Wings!
I am a satyr and a sodomite.
I am under the Shadow of the Wings!
I am as changeful and selfish as the sea.
I am under the Shadow of the Wings!
I am a thing of vice and vanity.
I am under the Shadow of the Wings!
I am most violent and I vacillate.
I am under the Shadow of the Wings!
I am a blind man and emasculate.
I am under the Shadow of the Wings!
I am a raging fire of wrath – no wiser.
I am under the Shadow of the Wings!
I am a blackguard, spendthrift and a miser.
I am under the Shadow of the Wings!
I am obscure and devious and null.
I am under the Shadow of the Wings!
I am ungenerous and base and dull.
I am under the Shadow of the Wings!
I am not marked with the white Flame of Breath.
I am under the Shadow of the Wings!
I am a traitor! – die the traitors death!
I am under the Shadow of the Wings!

Female form:

Yea! But I am a fool, and frivolous!
I am under the Shadow of the Wings!
I am a liar and a sorceress
I am under the Shadow of the Wings!
I am inconstant, I scorn the bridle!
I am under the Shadow of the Wings!
I am unchaste, voluptuous and idle.
I am under the Shadow of the Wings!
I am a harpy and an ogress crass.
I am under the Shadow of the Wings!
I am as dense and as stubborn as an ass.
I am under the Shadow of the Wings!
I am untrusty, cruel and insane.
I am under the Shadow of the Wings!
I am a fool and frivolous and vain.
I am under the Shadow of the Wings!
I am a weakling and a coward; I cringe.
I am under the Shadow of the Wings!
I am a lecheress and cunnilinge.
I am under the Shadow of the Wings!
I am a glutton, a besotted wight.
I am under the Shadow of the Wings!
I am a harlot and a sodomite.
I am under the Shadow of the Wings!
I am as changeful and selfish as the sea.
I am under the Shadow of the Wings!
I am a thing of vice and vanity.
I am under the Shadow of the Wings!
I am most violent and I vacillate.
I am under the Shadow of the Wings!
I am a woman blind and desolate.
I am under the Shadow of the Wings!

I am desperate and devoid of hope.
I am under the Shadow of the Wings!
I am a miscreant, spendthrift misanthrope.
I am under the Shadow of the Wings!
I am obscure and devious and null.
I am under the Shadow of the Wings!
I am ungenerous and base and dull.
I am under the Shadow of the Wings!
I am not marked with the white Flame of Breath.
I am under the Shadow of the Wings!
I am a traitor! – die the traitors death!
I am under the Shadow of the Wings!

(Immediately following the last line of the Confession the magician should rise to their feet as swiftly and keenly as may be).

(Then purify the circle with the prepared water and the sprinkler of mint, rosemary and marjoram, saying):

'Helel-O-Gaap; powerful Prince of water, aid me in sanctifying this Circle'.

(Then sprinkle blessed water around it, saying):

'In the Name of Nuit, and of Hadit, and of Ra Hoor Khu, Amen'.

Preliminary Invocations

These follow on from the Oath and Confession, and precede the Invocation of the appropriate deity.

(Immediately after purifying the circle with water burn an offering of Mace to the intermediary spirit of the True Grimoire, the spirit Scirlin, saying):

I burn this incense of Mace in the Name and to the Honour of Scirlin!'

(Then repeat his invocation seven times thus, displaying his sigil, and those of the spirits you intend to conjure):

HELOY ✠ TAU ✠ VARAF ✠ PANTHON
✠ HOMINORCUM ✠ ELEMIATH
✠ SERUGEATH ✠ AGLA ✠ ON ✠
TETRAGRAMMATON ✠ KAS-ALHI

If desired the last four names may be replaced with these A.M.E.N. Names: HOOR-APEP ✠ MAUT ✠ AOUIE ✠ AMMON-RA, or others of equivalent value. It is recommended that the conjuration that begins 'Astrachios, Asac, Asacro' be used in addition.

Then the Invocation of the Headless One in seven parts, found in The Magick of the Ghebers. Other forms of the same rite may be preferred. Both these rites are invocations of an intermediary between the magician and the world of gods and spirits. This procedure unifies the ritual approaches of the *True Grimoire*, African Traditional Religions, and the magic of many important and influential ancient cultures. Other related procedures and entities may be preferred, but it is important that this ritual phase itself be retained.

The Main Invocation follows, and at its climax the spirits sympathetic with the deity's nature are conjured. Although other Invocations may be equally appropriate, the Hekate Invocation is tailored for specifically this purpose. Accordingly, whereas the other invocations have a definite climax of their own and may be used independently of evocation, the climax of this invocation is the evocations.

THE INVOCATION OF HEKATE

I

I invoke Hekate, the Goddess of Witchcraft, the Lady of the Crossroads!

(If desired make Invoking Hexagram of the Moon with Divine Name QADOSH ISIS; and Sigil of the Moon with Divine Name MARY. Alternatively simply declare Names.)

O Thou Lady of the Darkest Night, Queen of the Earth, Sea and Sky – Diva Triformis, Tergemina, Triceps; Mediator of the realms. Thee, Thee, I invoke!

Thou who wearest the Crescent Moon for Thy diadem, on whose brow Shines the Sign of Thy Might! Thee, Thee, I invoke!

Thou adorned with the holy garland; Thee, Thee I invoke!

Thou, whose skin is of fairest white, whose hair shines with the Silver Moonlight. Thee, Thee, I invoke!

Thou in whose hand is the herald's wand of Hermes: Thee, Thee I invoke!

Thou who bearest the flame-bright torch. Thee, Thee, I invoke!

Thou at whose serpent girdle hangs the key to all realms: Thee, Thee, I invoke!

Thou whose sandal is of gleaming gold: Thee, Thee, I invoke!

Thou whose coming is heralded by the baying of dogs, Thee, Thee I invoke!

II

(Assume God-form of Hekate)

Behold! I am Kore, Mother and Hag!

I am Night and the Mother of Night, Sovereign Lady of Darkened Ways.

I am psychopomp, friend and guide to those who have passed.

My triform self traverses all worlds.

I open the Gates between all realms, for I hold and am the Key!

I bear the torch for those who have gone beyond – by my flame are they brought to Elysium.

Behold! She is in me & I in Her!

I am She: Goddess of the Crossroads – the Mother of Sorceries.

Traveller of the by-ways, knower of the heights of Olympus and of the depths of Hades!

For I am Hekate, the Mistress of Witchcraft.

I am the Maiden who hunts with Her hounds.

I am the Great Matron who watches over the child-bearing Mother.

I am the Hag who gives of Her ancient wisdom.

Mine are the charms of Witchcraft, and Mine the knowledge of Hidden sorceries.

My torch is the guidance of Demeter, sorrowing Eleusinian Mother.

For I have opened the Ways to and from Hades.

I mediate all planes.
I am the primeval Woman from whence you have come and to whom you shall return:

I am the Eternal guide of Gods and Men!

III

Therefore do Thou come forth from Thine Abode in the Silence: Supernal Wisdom! Dark and Deep!

ERESHKIGAL!
AKTIOPHIS!
NEBOUTOSOUALETH!

By whatsoever Name or Epithet Thou art called by all the Nations of the Earth, Thou art Nameless unto Eternity!

Thou who risest as the Maiden and Pregnant Moons! And the Wise Darkness of the Hag!

Thou Queen alike of all the realms, for Thou alone canst traverse them all!

Thou mate of Apollo, Phorcos and Aeetes, who bore Scylla, Circe and Medea, proud Sorceress of Old!

Thou knower of dread Hades' secret, Mistress of Witchcraft and Enchantment!

Thou, sole witness to the rape of Persephone, who didst lead Demeter to the Truth!

Thou, all-seeing and all-pervading Hekate Triforma!

Clothed in Darkest Night and Crowned with the Crescent Moon!

Come Thou forth I say, Come Thou forth! And make all spirits subject unto me, so that every spirit of the Firmament and of the Aethyr, on dry land and in the Water, upon the Earth or under the Earth, of Whirling Air or of Rushing Fire, and every Spell and Scourge of God the Vast One may be obedient unto me!

IV

I make open the Gates to all realms.

I ascend from Dark Hades;

I shine the light of my Crescent Diadem upon you
My Children gathered together at my Holy Crossroads!

Virgin, bitch, serpent, key, herald's wand, Golden sandal
of the Lady of Tartaros!

I have been initiated;
I have descended to the Chamber of the Autocthons;

I have seen the Holy Things!
I call upon you who have all forms and many names,
Double-horned goddess, Mene. Whose form none
knows save IAO alone, Creator of the Universe;
Who shaped you into the 28 shapes of the world.

Thus do you complete every form and distribute breath
to every living thing that it might flourish. Thou who
waxest from obscurity into light, and diminisheth into
darkness.

The first companion of your name is Silence,
The second a popping sound,
The third a low groaning,
The fourth a sustained hissing,
The fifth a cry of joy!
The sixth a moaning noise,
The seventh as the barking of dogs;
The eighth a mighty bellowing;

The ninth as the neighing of horses.
The tenth a musical sound,
The eleventh a sounding wind,
The twelfth a wind creating sound,
The thirteenth a sound of coercion:
The ultimate a coercive emanation from Perfection!

Ox, vulture, bull, beetle, falcon, crab, dog,
Wolf, serpent, horse, she-goat, asp, kid, he-goat,
Baboon, cat, lion, leopard, fieldmouse, deer, multiform,
Virgin, torch, lightning, garland, heralds wand, child,
key!

I have spoken your signs and the symbols of your name
that you might hear me, Mistress of the World, Stable
One, Mighty One!

THE CONJURATION OF ASTAROTH

A-A SA TA A-A RA OA TA HA
SA KA ASI SA U GA ASI ZA
TA ASI MALAE E AIWAZ NU ASAR-ISA ANKH
A-A SA TA A-A RA OA TA HA
RA U AIWAZ RA LAM ASAR AMN OAZ
OA GA NU OA ASAR O-O IAO ASAR-ISA HAD
TA ASI ASAR-ISA E AIWAZ NU ASAR-ISA ANKH
HA ZA GU HA OAZ HAD ANKH OA:
Come, ASTAROTH ✠ AMEN ✠

(Display the sigil and offer incense saying):

 I offer this incense in the Name of and to the honour
of Astaroth;

(Greet the spirit):

Do what thou wilt shall be the whole of the Law! I greet you the powerful Chief: Astaroth, and salute you in the Name of the Lord of the Aeon, Ra Hoor Khu. I am right pleased that thou hast come in answer to the Sacred Rites, and ask that thou direct thy spirit Nebiros - whom we conjure - to attend our call. In the Names of Nuit, Hadit and of Ra Hoor Khuit, So Mote it Be, Amen.

(When you have spoken with Astaroth and she has granted your request, make the following invitation before proceeding to conjure Nebiros):

I thank thee Astaroth for thy powerful assistance,
Abide here and share our feast.

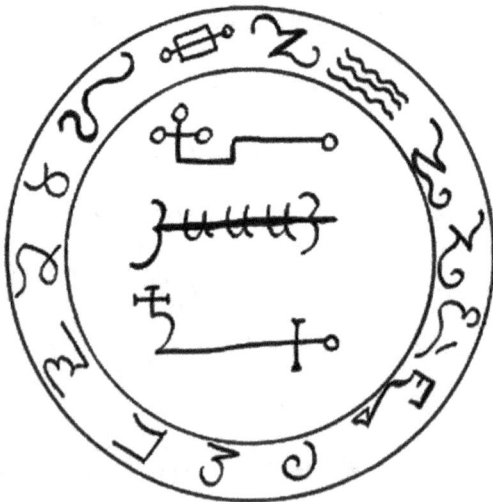

THE CONJURATION OF NEBIROS

(or other deputy as appropriate)

'I call upon you, holy, very-powerful, very-glorious, very-strong, holy, autocthons; assistants of the great God, the powerful chief daimons; you who are inhabitants of Chaos, of Erebos, of the abyss, of the depth, of earth, dwelling in the recesses of heaven, lurking in the nooks and crannies of houses, shrouded in dark clouds; watchers of things not to be seen, guardians of secrets; leaders of those in the underworld, administrators of the infinite, wielding power over earth; earth-shakers, foundation-layers, servants in the chasm, shudderful fighters, fearful ministers, turning the spindle, freeing snow and rain, air-transversers, causing summer heat, wind-bringers, lords of Fate, inhabitants of dark Erebos, bringers of compulsion, sending flames of fire, bringing snow and dew, wind-releasers, disturbers of the deep, treaders on the calm sea, mighty in courage, grievers of the heart, powerful potentates, cliff-walkers, adverse demons, iron-hearted, wild-tempered, unruly, guarding Tartaros, misleading Fate, all-seeing, all-hearing, all-subjecting, heaven-walkers, spirit-givers, ever existing, heaven-shakers, gladdening the heart, those who join together death, revealers of angels, punishers of mortals, sunless revealers, rulers of daimons, air-transversers, almighty, holy, unconquerable AOTH ABAOTH BASUM ISAK SABAOTH IAO! ABRASAZAZ - A - ABRA, HUA, AMEN. O RA-HOOR-KHUIT, AIWAZ, RA! Come: Nebiros Come: ✠ AMEN ✠

(*Display the sigil and offer incense saying*):

I offer this incense in the Name of and to the honour of Nebiros.

(*Greet him saying*):

Do what thou wilt shall be the whole of the Law! I greet you the powerful ruling spirit, Nebiros, and salute you in the Name of the Lord of the Aeon, Ra Hoor Khu. I am right pleased that thou hast come in answer to the Sacred Rites, and ask that thou direct thy spirits N and N and N - whom we conjure - to attend our call. In the Name of Nuit, Hadit and of Ra Hoor Khuit. So Mote it Be. Amen.

(*When you have spoken with Nebiros, and he has granted your request, prior to proceeding to conjure subordinate spirits make the same invitation as before*).

ANOTHER CONJURATION
for subordinates of Nebiros:

I conjure thee, N..., by the authority of Hekate, by the power of Astaroth and of Nebiros, to attend here and (here state what you require from the spirit) by the power of the Holy and Sacred Names of Nuit, Hadit, Ra-Hoor-Khuit.

(*Display the sigil and offer incense as before. When you have spoken with them and they have granted your request, then if appropriate, prior to beginning the closing ceremony, make the same invitation as before*).

THE RITUAL OF THE PYRAMID:
SOUTH WEST VARIANT

The Building of the Pyramid.

(The Magus with Wheel Wand. On the Altar are Water & the Oil. In the left hand is the Bell.)

'Hail, Set-Hor! Hail, Thoth! Let
The Silence speech beget!'

(Two strokes on the Bell. Banishing spiral dance.)

'The Key of Asi flashing here
Embraceth each revolving Sphere,
Touching and entering all, to hold
The Sign that tears the veil asunder;
O Woman clothed with Solar gold.
Sebek is smitten by the Thunder
The Light breaks forth from under!

(Go to the place between the stations of Tahuti and Hoor-Apep, and face SW.)

'South Western Angle of the Plane,
Moon Crowned Queen bearing the Wheel
On serpent coiled wand; again
Bring honey, oil, red wine and meal
To our anointed Feast of Light
In joy and beauty, work the Rite'

(Lay the Wheeled Wand etc. on the altar, and douse head saying:)

'The Lustral Water! Smite thy flood
Through me lymph, marrow & blood!'

(*Anointing, say:*)

'The Fire Informing! Let the Oil
Balance, assain, assoil!'

(*The Invoking Spiral Dance with wanded wheel*)

'Disorder holds the wheel, & runs
Whirling amid the Suns.
Hail Set! Pace the Path, thy spear
Makes the path of Ra's boat clear!'

(*Sign of the Mourning of Isis:*)

'Homage to Thee, Lady of Love!'

(*Sign of Isis Rejoicing:*)

'Lady of Light, Homage to Thee!'

(*Repeat both Signs:*)

'Thee we adore, still & stirred
 Beyond Infinity.'

(*The Secret Word.*)

'......'

'For as the Turning of the Wheel
And the Silence of the Fire

The Beyond here and now reveal,
As thou hast power to inspire.
This is the Path of HUA   Ho!
This is the path of IAO.'

(*Bell.*)

'Hail Hoor Apep Thou Sword of Steel!
Alpha & Delta kissed & came
For Five that feed the Flame.'

(*Bell.*)

'Hail, Thrice Great! Serpent staff, winged heel
Alpha & Delta and Epsilon
Met in the Shadow of the Pylon
And in Iota did proclaim
That tenfold core & crown of flame.
Hail, Thoth and Thy Thrice Great fame!'

(*Thus is the Great Pyramid duly builded.*)

The Sealing of the Pyramid.

(*The Magus with Wheeled Wand. On the Altar are Water &
the Oil. In the
left hand is the Bell.*)

'Hail, Set-Hor! Hail, Thoth! Let
The Silence speech beget!'

(*Two strokes on the Bell. Banishing spiral dance.*)

'The Key of Asi flashing here

Embraceth each revolving Sphere,
Touching and entering all, to hold
The Sign that tears the veil asunder;
O Woman clothed with Solar gold.
Sebek is smitten by the Thunder
The Light breaks forth from under!

*(Go to the place between the stations of Tahuti and Hoor-
Apep, and face SW.)*

'South Western Angle of the Plane,
Moon Crowned Queen bearing the Wheel
On serpent coiled wand; again
Bring honey, oil, red wine and meal
To our anointed Feast of Light
In joy and beauty, work the Rite'

*(lay the Wheeled Wand etc. on the altar, and douse head
saying:)*

'The Lustral Water! Smite thy flood
Through me lymph, marrow & blood!

(Anointing the Wounds, say:)

'The Fire Informing! Let the Oil
Balance, assain, assoil!'

The Banishing Spiral Dance

'Disorder holds the wheel, & runs
Whirling amid the Suns.
Hail Set! Pace the Path, reverse
Thy circuit of the Universe!

(Sign of the Mourning of Isis:)

'Homage to Thee, Lady of Love!'

(Sign of Isis Rejoicing:)

'Lady of Light, Homage to Thee!'

(Repeat both Signs:)

'Thee we adore, still & stirred
 Beyond Infinity.'

(The Secret Word.)

'......'

(The Eucharist at the Altar)

'Behold the Perfect One hath said
These are my body's elements
tried & found pure, a golden spoil.'

(Act accordingly.)

'Incense and Wine and Fire and Bread
These I consume, true Sacraments,
For the Perfection of the Oil
For I am clothed about with flesh
And I am the Eternal Spirit.
I am the Lord that riseth fresh
From Death, whose glory I inherit
Since I partake with him. I am
The manifestor of the Unseen,

Without me all the land of Khem
Is as if it had not been'

(If any spirits have been conjured in the performance of
this ritual, offer
them the elements of the sacrament, naming the spirits
and saying:

Share with me this fine perfume,
This portion of the wine consume,
Enjoy the warmth of holy fire,
This bread receive e'er thee retire.)

Only then make the license to depart:

Depart thee in peace unto thine habitations, and be there ever
peace between
me and thee, and be ye ever ready to come when thou art called,
either by a
Word, or by a Will, or by the Sacred Rites of Magick.)

'For as the Turning of the Wheel
And the Silence of the Fire

The Beyond here and now reveal,
As thou hast power to inspire.
This is the Path of HUA   Ho!
This is the path of IAO.'

(Bell.)

'Hail Hoor Apep Thou Sword of Steel!
Alpha & Delta kissed & came
For Five that feed the Flame.'

(Bell.)

'Hail, Thrice Great! Serpent staff, winged heel
Alpha & Delta and Epsilon
Met in the Shadow of the Pylon
And in Iota did proclaim
That tenfold core & crown of flame.
Hail, Thoth and Thy Thrice Great fame!'

Hail, Hoor! Hail Asi! Hail Tahuti! Hail,
Asar Un Nefer! through the rendered veil.
I am Thyself, with all Thy brilliance decked

Khabs Am Pekht.'

(Thus is the Great Pyramid duly sealed.)

OFFERINGS

1. By the burning of the incense was the Word revealed,
and by the distant drug.
2. O meal and honey and oil! O beautiful flag of the
moon, that she hangs out in the centre of bliss!
The Book of Lapis Lazuli; chapter VII.

Two kinds of offering were mentioned in the course of
describing the Invocation of Hecate as a rite of evocation.
Reference was made to an offering of incense at the arrival
of each spirit, and also to an invitation to share in the
sacrament which forms part of the conclusion of these rituals.
As this procedure becomes familiar various refinements
follow from these. First and foremost is the acceptability of
various types of offering to deities and spirits. To a degree
this is a matter of research for individuals, whether through
academic routes or through divination. However it would
be irresponsible of me not to make at least a preliminary
examination of the matter. Having embarked upon which,
further considerations swiftly come to light.

Those readers who are not self avowed thelemites, or
who while sympathetic are offended by hard-line approaches,
need not be dismayed at my involving the *Holy Books of
Thelema* in this discussion at various points. When I do it
is not from a 'hard-line' position, but simply to continue
the integrated analysis of conjuring through liturgical
procedures. The simple fact is that *The Book of the Law*, and
the other 'Class A' texts, happen to mention virtually all the
substances used as offerings in ancient 'Western' paganism.
This facilitates an unfamiliar but valuable approach to these
texts which departs almost immediately from what has

become 'mainstream' Thelema; as such it may well be more
readily grasped by people from other traditions entirely,
which is probably no coincidence.

Besides the mention of resinous woods and gums in
the first chapter of *AL* there is a more comprehensive list
in the third. Meal and honey are mentioned, both of which
were standard offerings in ancient Greece; meal generally
indicating barley rather than wheat. Wine is mentioned, as
are two kinds of oil; the aromatic Abramelin oil and plain
olive oil. Wine and olive oil were both widely employed in
sacrificial rites, in which aromatic oils were also used. Most
of these substances were standard offerings; barley meal was
an almost invariable part of any offering. Wine on the other
hand although widely used was subject to some restrictions,
particularly with older deities, of a chthonic nature, whose
cult predated its use. One widely used sacramental substance
not specifically mentioned in the *Book of the Law* is milk;
which appears in Liber VII and Liber LXV.

The other important sacramental substance specified
in *AL* of course, is blood. Animal sacrifice is referred to at
various points, as is bloodletting and the use of menstrual
blood; all in a sacramental and/or sacrificial context. This is
a controversial area, and one which I do not propose to enter
into fully in print for various reasons. What is relevant here
is that, despite its importance in other contexts, in the first
chapter of *AL* the use of blood is emphatically prohibited
for those rituals concerning the Star Goddess; which can be
extended to include most rituals of an astrological nature.
The references to milk elsewhere in the *Holy Books* then
gain additional significance, for those references involve the
goddess of the stars.

Two other sacramental substances, if we may call
them this, appear in the *Book of the Law*, namely Fire and
Water. Both of these are important in ancient contexts. Fire

was intimately involved with most kinds of offering rite, whether as a vehicle of burnt offerings, or as an offering in its own right. Water similarly was a vehicle for the making of offerings, cast into rivers and lakes etc., as well as a sacramental substance in its own right.

It is not my intention to elaborate further on what the significance of these substances may be in the context of an inner mystery of Thelemic texts. However it will interest some if we quickly consider their numeration with the gematria system known as the English Qaballa.

SACRAMENT	EQ VALUE
Fire	78
Water	65
Wine	65
Honey	65
Meal	49
Blood	42
Milk	55
Oil	32

OFFERINGS TO GODS AND SPIRITS

To return to our ritual: each spirit is initially greeted and honoured with an offering of incense. Until otherwise informed in the process of negotiation with such spirits the assumption is that this will be frankincense. This assumption is based on various considerations. In the first place, while the *True Grimoire* mentions several distinct incenses for various purposes, it specifies frankincense for greeting spirits. Secondly, while little appreciated by many ceremonial magicians, some grimoires – the *True Grimoire* included – are essentially guides to beginning magical work with the spirits concerned with some useful additional advice; they are not a comprehensive manual for everything which follows. In other words the grimoire 'introduces' the magician to a spirit or spirits by traditional formalities, which having been achieved they are meant to get to know one another. In the course of which the individual spirit will either inform the magician of their likes and dislikes, or will be asked! Do not assume – for example – that because you are interested in a particular spirit for reasons concerning love that a generic incense of Venus will serve. Offer frankincense at the first meeting, and then go on to discover if the spirit would prefer benzoin or sandalwood, or something quite unexpected. In my work some spirits remain content with frankincense, others specify additional ingredients.

This kind of offering obviously involves 'resinous woods and gums', and also fire. I have also learned by experience – subsequently supported by historical precedent – that the spirits of the *True Grimoire* respond best when an offering of fire, for example a candle or small pyre, is included in the offerings. This is almost an invariable rule, although again there may be individual exceptions, a possibility the magician should always be alert to.

Another possibility to be alert to, particularly in dealings with spirits from the papyri and archaic Goetia, involves meal. A sprinkling of this on the ground when greeting such spirits is likely to be well received, and may be extended to the sacramental phase of the ritual as well. Often such sprinkling occurs after the pouring of libations, which might consist of any or almost all of the liquids mentioned here, although blood is generally distinct from the others. The barley meal is then sprinkled over the spilled liquid. Following similar traditions the heads of sacrificial victims, if any, may be sprinkled with meal in the same way. In a similar vein the bread of the sacrament may be replaced by a barley cake. Such offerings are also appropriate to some of the older Greek deities; who in their pre-Olympian guise are as appropriate to these rituals as any Egyptian deity.

Such archaic deities and their attendant spirits may also be averse to wine. Barley beer is an appropriate and readily obtained substitute. It is important to note that beer was a frequent offering in Egyptian rituals, those of Set included; it is also preferred by many Greek chthonic deities. Symbolically and magically such substitutions may still be considered and referred to as 'wine' in the context of these rituals; although alternative rhyming sections could be composed if desired.

Honey is a frequent offering in Greek ritual, mixed with water it forms a sacramental substance known as *nephalia*, or if fermented as *hydromel*; it is also used in making sacramental bread and cakes. In goetic rites it is useful to add some to water offerings when dealing with the 'harder' or 'hotter' types of spirit in order to 'sweeten' them. Hydromel is obviously another important substitute for wine, although some rites might include nephalia and wine.

Oil, whether olive or aromatic, is a frequent ingredient of offerings, although often treated differently from other liquids. Milk, oil and honey are very appropriate offerings for spirits of woodland, among others; wine, honey and milk to ancient spirits of the dead. As is evident oil may be poured as a libation, or used for anointing. Some spirits respond to the use of aromatic oil much as others do to honey, pacifying them or preventing unwanted demonstrations.

Water is a very traditional sacramental substance, although old hands – and careful readers of some of my other writings – will be aware that water obtained from different sources has a range of different associations. Speaking generally, sometimes water is the only liquid offering made, while on other occasions it follows the other liquid offerings.

Having thus swiftly dealt with many of the various substances employed in offerings to spirits, and to the deities associated with them, some final points remain. In particular it would be irresponsible, and also disrespectful, to neglect to deal with the more controversial or exciting kinds of offering.

It will be recalled that I excused myself dealing with animal sacrifice in any depth. In keeping with the direction of the notes above I should nevertheless mention that traditionally chthonic offerings of this kind are made with the head of the animal facing downwards, and in celestial offerings facing up. Similarly, chthonic offerings were made in their entirety; no portion of the animal was reserved for feasting after the rite. However, in a modern context it is by no means unusual to hear one of two comments regarding these practices:

Firstly, there is the practitioner who says they prefer to offer sexual substances rather than blood. Then there are those who delight in offering both. In the context of dealing properly with spirits, I am sorry to say, the preferences of the operator are secondary. The individual operator may have a taste for bloodletting or sexual ritual or indeed both. It is nevertheless wise to ascertain that this kind of offering is what the spirit wants! At the beginning of my workings with the spirits of the *True Grimoire* I was fully expecting to make blood offerings, and perfectly willing to do so. However, having worked with over thirty of these spirits over the course of some years, the amount of times I have been asked for blood are negligible, although significant. Judging by my experience the most suitable occasions are at the beginning of relations with them, or important times thereafter.

Secondly, there is the advice occasionally heard that you should never, never offer spirits blood, as they will then demand it more and more. As the reader will have judged from the advice above, this has not been my experience with these particular spirits.

Much the same remarks apply to the offering of sexual substances, although in this respect these spirits have less interest than in blood, where as said though rare the incidences remain significant.

Although the title of 'demons' is relevant enough, the chiefs governing this hierarchy are evolved and sentient creatures. The most important offerings for these spirits are the performance of ritual, and fire. The operator would be well advised to deal with them respectfully, and pay attention to their desires. While usually fairly readily called and worked with there will be occasions where the work becomes extremely demanding. The foolish, arrogant or heavy handed operator will be hard pressed to deal with such situations. Do not expect a sharp knife and the names of an uncaring God to deliver you from their clutches if you treat them badly, or expect something for nothing.

PART II

THE INVOCATION OF TAHUTI

AS MAY ALREADY BE CLEAR TO SOME READERS, MY MAIN INTEREST in traditional Thelemic ritual is centred on those elements with a Greco-Egyptian emphasis. These are more compatible with elements from the magical papyri, and in turn with my 'liturgical transplant', i.e. adapting *Verum* from the Judaeo-Christian paradigm in which most grimoires were recast from the Greco-Roman synthesis underlying most Western magic.

These rituals comprise: *Liber Pyramidos*, *Liber Israfel*, the *Invocation of Horus*, the *Bornless* or *Headless Rite* and the *Adorations of the Sun* in *Liber Resh vel Helios*.

In this section is presented the most straightforward example of the use of the Opening and Closing sub-rituals from *Pyramidos* as a frame for a rite of Invocation. The invocation in this case is the Invocation of Tahuti from *Liber Israfel*. This rite is also known as 'Majesty of Godhead', since the actual invocation in *Israfel*, when shorn of preliminaries and extras, begins with those words. It is accordingly a simple matter to replace the 'preliminaries and extras' with the Opening and Closing of the Pyramid and the adjuncts of evocation described in the previous instalment. From the combination of these elements developed the entire liturgical approach outlined in this book. Thus the Invocation of Tahuti within this framework is illustrative of the whole approach.

Understanding and performance of this Invocation, and others of which it is a premier example, may be greatly enhanced by reference to Crowley's *Magick*, Book II Chapter II – *The Formula of the Elemental Weapons*. Here he details that the first part of the invocation commemorates the physical attributes of the god, enabling a clear mental picture to be built up. The second part is as it were the voice of the god making his characteristic utterance. The third part asserts the identity of the magician with the deity. The fourth part is as it were uttered by the god invoking themselves, as if it were their will to manifest to the magician. After this the purpose of the invocation is stated, which is often a conjuration of a spirit or spirits of a similar nature to the deity concerned; in this case Lucifer, his deputies and their subordinates.

In my opinion a pre-existing relationship of *Israfel* and *Pyramidos* is readily detectable. This is particularly exhibited by the otherwise unexplained appearance of Asi, prominent in the latter, towards the end of the former:

> I invoke the priestess of the Silver Star, Asi the Curved One, by the ritual of Silence.
> 'I make open the gate of Bliss; I descend from the Palace of the Stars; I greet you, I embrace you, O children of Earth, that are gathered together in the Hall of Darkness.'

APPLIED COSMOLOGY IN PYRAMIDOS

In the first part of this book the use of *Pyramidos* as the basis for Invocation and Evocation rites was introduced. The essential principles of this approach involve correlation of the three points of the 'Pyramid' and their gods with the three chiefs of the *Grimorium Verum*. This is greatly facilitated by the similar floor-plans of the *Verum* circle (Fig. 1) and the temple layout of *Pyramidos* (Fig. 1).

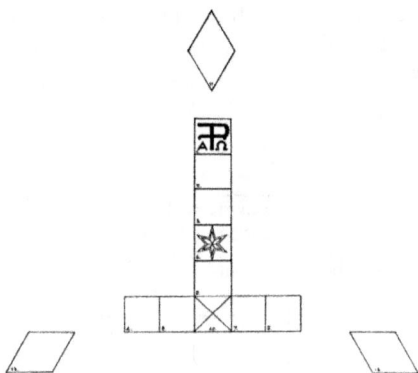

FIG. 1.
The Triangle of the Universe.

FIG. 2
Goetic circle.

The three points of the internal triangle of the goetic circle correspond to the directions personified in *Pyramidos* by three deities, who in turn represent the highest expression of the forces ruled by the three chiefs of the *Verum* system, thus:

DIRECTION	MEANING	EGYPTIAN GODFORM	GREEK EQUIVALENT	CHIEF SPIRIT
East	Balance	Tahuti	Hermes Kthonios	Lucifer
South-West	Life	Asi	Persephone or Hecate	Astaroth
North-West	Death	Hoor-Apep	Hades or Dis Pater	Belzebuth

The 'Egyptian' forms of these names in this schema require some comment: Tahuti is the pre-eminent magician god, also known as Thoth and as Hermes Trismegistus; Asi is a 'poetic' Egyptian form of Isis; Hoor-Apep represents a unification of the twin gods Horus and Set. As shown in my *Headless One (Equinox BJoT VII 6)* this combined form is authentically Egyptian as well as important within Thelemic cosmology.

While this ritual derives from Thelemic sources it should be well understood that the trinity of gods employed has much older predecessors. The ritual can in fact be employed regardless of whether the magician is an adherent of Thelema or not.

For example, the triad can be readily identified as Egyptian equivalents of Hermes Kthonios (the Underworld form of Hermes), Persephone or Hecate, and Hades or Dis Pater. Hermes, Demeter and Hades are implicit in *Pyramidos* prior to my usage; their Greek initials figure in the Opening and Closing.

These are particularly important deities in Greek and Greco-Egyptian magic and archaic goetia; the rulers of the Underworld and their messenger or psychopomp, the 'Guide of Souls'. The ritual modus operandi here delineated can therefore be employed in a huge variety of workings. As well as the conjuration of spirits from the grimoire the magician has the additional option of employing this ritual in conjunction with elements drawn from the Greco-Egyptian Magical Papyri. Thorough ongoing investigation of the ritual in these forms will also reveal how closely allied these options are.

It should also be firmly born in mind that there are differences in effect as well as emphasis between Pyramidos and the two variants. These effects go beyond the particular purpose for which the ritual is performed on any given occasion.

Generally speaking the Invocation of Tahuti – and the conjuration of Lucifer – imply balance and are without significant side effects other than a general enhancement of the magician's life and development.

The invocation of Isis or Hecate, and the conjuration of Astaroth, emphasises Life. Since Life and Death are a polarity, emphasis on one without the other involves imbalance. Performance of this ritual thus has side effects which while generally desirable are not in balance. Peak experiences may follow quite swiftly, of an extraordinary kind, requiring careful assimilation. An account of such a 'side effect' forms a part of my account of the conjuration of Nebiros in a forthcoming book from Scarlet Imprint.

The invocation of Hoor-Apep (in whatever form) implies death, and powerful negative side effects may follow. The forces involved in this ritual are 'hotter' or 'harder'; they are difficult to mediate and far less forgiving of lapses in procedure, regardless of mitigating circumstances. In addition they are primarily destructive, and may negate unconstructive influences in the magician's life to which the magician is nevertheless strongly drawn or attached. It is of course understood that dire warnings of this kind are frequently ignored or undervalued. The magician would nevertheless be well advised not to attempt this form of the ritual without careful preparation and considerable experience.

PRACTICAL CONSIDERATIONS

I – BUILDING OF GODFORMS

The original form of *Pyramidos* involved Tahuti as the focus of the rite in the East, with Isis and Hoor-Apep representing twin poles in SW and NW. Within the existing Thelemic liturgy *Pyramidos* was developed to serve a dual function. The rite in its entirety is an initiation ritual of A∴A∴. In addition *Pyramidos* contains sub rituals which Crowley employed in composing rituals of invocation, as in the *Paris Working* and elsewhere. It is the second aspect of the ritual which is developed and illustrated in this section. Our introductory instalment introduced the concept of variant rituals attributed to SW and NW giving an example of the former. In this second part the original rite is examined in this role, while in that to follow the remaining variant will be introduced and its applications analysed and illustrated.

The god of the Eastern station of the temple in this rite is Tahuti; his attributes are rehearsed in the short invocation in the Opening rite:

'O Thou, the Apex of the Plane,
With Ibis head and Phoenix Wand
And Wings of Night! Whose serpents strain
Their bodies, bounding the Beyond.
Thou in the Light & in the Night
Art One, above their moving might!'

This invocation enables the magician to swiftly build up an image of the god in the East. The main invocation which follows the Opening develops the same approach, with a more detailed rehearsal of attributes. This balancing of a short and long invocation within the same ritual has a partial parallel in another important Thelemic ritual, namely the *Invocation of Horus*. In that ritual too there is a short rhyming invocation of Horus:

> Strike, strike the Master Chord
> Draw, Draw the Flaming Sword
> Crowned Child and Conquering Lord
> Horus, Avenger!

These 'short invocations' should be seen as models of a type, which can be used independently in a variety of roles.

Incidentally the *Invocation of Horus* is one that can readily be performed with the NW variant of *Pyramidos* as its 'frame'. This particular variant will be explored in the next instalment.

II – THE SECRET WORD

The 'Secret Word' in *Pyramidos* is capable of several layers of interpretation. In the original script it was encoded using colours from *Liber 777* as fairly transparent cipher substitutes for Hebrew letters. This is easily decoded as M Tz T B Tz M (made pronounceable by adding the vowel following the initial of each Hebrew letter: Metzatabetzam), the Tarot Trumps corresponding in Hermetic Qabalah symbolise the key stages of *Pyramidos*. On another level this word itself is a substitute for the 'Password' of the Neophyte grade in A∴A∴.

All of this is very recondite and interesting in its way, while on a more immediate and practical level it is not particularly significant. Magicians can substitute other words appropriate to the task in hand, or to their overall work. While 'Abrahadabra' is perhaps the best such general word, Names of Power relevant to spirits conjured in the ceremony are good 'task related' options. An inkling of these can be found in the *Path of the Names* in the previous issue. In my own work I have used both Abrahadabra and more specific names derived from gematria analysis of the Trees of Eternity.

III – THE OATH AND CONFESSION

As will be noted by careful readers, the version of *Pyramidos* presented here differs in some respects from the original. Chief among these is the omission of the self-inflicted wounds and the employment of scourge, dagger and chain (although the description of these in *MTP* remains important and is recommended to all practicing magicians, I prefer to interpret them as allegorical). In place of these is the dousing of the head with cold water, inspired by a classical description of an Isis invocation in the *Golden Ass*.

The combination of *Verum* elements and *Pyramidos* has another consequence of similar import. The Confession phase of the ritual involves the raising and lowering of two wands alternately while in a position of abasement. This is deeply suggestive of a rite of auto-flagellation. It is important to bear in mind in this respect that flagellation was substituted for human sacrifice in ancient Sparta. The confession therefore involves a powerful physical, emotional and psychic stimulus; this is of central importance as a practical technique within the recitation of the ritual.

As the Confession and a variant form thereof were included in the previous issue they are omitted from the script here, and are simply indicated by a title between *Opening* and *Invocation*. While superficially one might interpret the

Confession as a Christian idea, it is fully recognised, and its employment recommended in Crowley's description of ritual in *MTP III 15*. This chapter is also therefore recommended as further reading.

IV – THE EUCHARIST AT THE ALTAR

The ritual of initiation that is the original form of *Pyramidos* as a whole involves an additional god besides the three so far alluded to. The station occupied by this god is the topmost point of a 'pyramid' (in the form of a tetrahedron) of which the triangular floor-plan of the ritual forms the base. The god subsequently descends from this point to occupy the temple when it is properly builded, and this is celebrated in the Eucharist.

This god is Osiris, more properly Asar-Un-Nefer, the Perfected Man; he is, in Thelemic terms, no longer the Hierophant as of old but the higher self of the Candidate. The Eucharist therefore is a magical Mass; it is both 'pagan' and comparable with Gnostic Christianity.

The magician who performs the Eucharist signals their intention of performing the Great Work, or commemorates actual union with their 'Angel' (the Task of an Adeptus Minor). While derived from the Neophyte ritual, in practice *Pyramidos* can initiate into all three grades mentioned in the *Book of the Law*, (0=0, 5=6 and 8=3).

In all the variants of the ritual the god of the Eucharist remains the same; Osiris as slain god, who was thus also Lord of the Underworld. In *Liber Tau* – which forms a profound commentary on the triadic nature of Thelemic initiation and ritual – we read 'Asar as Bull, as Man, As Sun', these forms relate to the three grades above mentioned, in the same order. The Greek equivalent of this Eucharistic god is Dionysus, the god of divine madness or inspiration. It thus reflects initiatory traditions intimately associated with archaic goetia.

The remarks on appropriate offerings in the previous issue should be carefully examined when deciding to retain or substitute the various items of which the Eucharist consists. So long as adaptation or substitution is sensitively done the four elements of the Mass will retain their main symbolism when adapted to the purposes of one performance or another. Fire should always be present when working with the spirits of the *True Grimoire*; the incense, wine and bread may be adapted or substituted according to the known preferences of individual spirits (but only once this is ascertained directly).

If these elements of the rite are well understood the ritual and its variants becomes readily worked by any ritualist; their own experience will supply further insight and enhancement. The ritual itself deserves to become part of the repertoire of any serious magician either empathic with the Thelemic cosmology or seeking to operate within a reconstructed Greco-Egyptian frame. This obviously includes modern pagan magicians uncomfortable with the Judaeo-Christian cast of the grimoires while simultaneously attracted to them.

THE RITUAL OF THE PYRAMID:
EAST

(The Magus with Wand. On the Altar are Incense, Fire, Bread, Wine. The bell is held in the left hand.)

'Hail, Asi! Hail, Hoor Apep! Let
The Silence speech beget!'

(Two strokes on the Bell. Banishing spiral dance.)

'The Words against the Son of Night.
Tahuti speaketh in the Light
Knowledge and Power, twin warriors shake
The Invisible; they roll asunder
The darkness; matter shines, a snake.
Sebek is smitten by the thunder
The Light breaks forth from Under.'

(The Magus goes to the West, in the centre of the base of the Pyramid of Thoth, Asi, and Hoor.)

'O Thou, the Apex of the Plane,
With Ibis head and Phoenix Wand
And Wings of Night! Whose serpents strain
Their bodies, bounding the Beyond.
Thou in the Light & in the Night
Art One, above their moving might!'

(Lay the Wand on the altar, and douse head saying:):

'The Lustral Water! Smite thy flood
Through me lymph, marrow & blood!'

(*Anointing, say*):

'The Fire Informing! Let the Oil
Balance, assain, assoil!'

The Invoking Spiral Dance

'So Life takes Fire from Death, & runs
Whirling amid the Suns.
Hail Asi! Pace the Path, bind on
The girdle of the Starry One!'

(*Sign of the Enterer*):

'Homage to Thee, Lord of the Word!'

(*Sign of Silence*):

'Lord of Silence, Homage to Thee!'

(*Repeat both Signs*):

'Lord, we adore Thee, still & stirred
 Beyond Infinity.'

(*The Secret Word.*)

'......'

'For from the Silence of the Wand
Unto the Speaking of the Sword.
And back again to the Beyond,
This is the toil & the Reward
This is the Path of HUA   Ho!

This is the path of IAO.'

(*Bell.*)

'Hail Asi! Hail, thou Wanded Wheel!
Alpha & Delta kissed & came
For Five that feed the Flame.'

(*Bell.*)

'Hail, Hoor-Apep! thou Sword of Steel!
Alpha & Delta and Epsilon
Met in the Shadow of the Pylon
And in Iota did proclaim
That tenfold core & crown of flame.
Hail, Hoor-Apep! Unspoken Name!'

(*Thus is the Great Pyramid duly builded.*)

(Oath and Confession – see part one)

INVOCATION OF TAHUTI

I

O Thou! Majesty of Godhead! Wisdom-crowned Tahuti!
Lord of the Gates of the Universe! Thee, Thee, I invoke.
O Thou of the Ibis Head! Thee, Thee I invoke.
Thou who wieldest the Wand of Double Power! Thee,
Thee I invoke!
Thou who bearest in Thy left hand the Rose and Cross
of Light and Life: Thee, Thee, I invoke.
Thou, whose head is as an emerald, and Thy nemmes as
the night-sky blue! Thee, Thee I invoke.

Thou, whose skin is of flaming orange as though it burned in a furnace! Thee, Thee I invoke.

II

Behold! I am Yesterday, To-Day, and the Brother of To-Morrow!
I am born again and and again.
Mine is the Unseen Force, whereof the Gods are sprung! Which is as Life unto the Dwellers in the Watch-Towers of the Universe.
I am the Charioteer of the East, Lord of the Past and of the Future.
I see by mine own inward light: Lord of Resurrection; Who cometh forth from the Dusk, and my birth is from the House of Death.
O ye two Divine Hawks upon your Pinnacles!
Who keep watch over the Universe!
Ye who company the Bier to the House of Rest!
Who pilot the Ship of Ra advancing onwards to the heights of heaven!
Lord of the Shrine which standeth in the Centre of the Earth!

III

Behold, He is in me, and I in Him!
Mine is the Radiance, wherein Ptah floateth over the firmament!
I travel upon high!
I tread upon the firmament of Nu!
I raise a flashing flame, with the lightning of Mine Eye!
Ever rushing on, in the splendour of the daily glorified Ra: giving my life to the Dwellers of Earth.

If I say "Come up upon the mountains!" the Celestial Waters shall flow at my Word.
For I am Ra incarnate!
Khephra created in the Flesh!
I am the Eidolon of my father Tmu, Lord of the City of the Sun!
The God who commands is in my mouth!
The God of Wisdom is in my Heart!
My tongue is the Sanctuary of Truth!
And a God sitteth upon my lips.
My Word is accomplished every day!
And the desire of my heart realises itself, as that of Ptah when He createth!
I am Eternal; therefore all things are as my designs; therefore do all things obey my Word.

IV

Therefore do Thou come forth unto me from Thine abode in the Silence:
Unutterable Wisdom! All-Light! All-Power!
Thoth! Hermes! Mercury! Odin!
By whatever name I call Thee, Thou art still nameless to Eternity:. Come Thou forth, I say, and aid and guard me in this work of Art.

Thou, Star of the East, that didst conduct the Magi!
Thou art The Same all-present in Heaven and in Hell!
Thou that vibratest between the Light and the Darkness!
Rising, descending! Changing ever, yet ever The Same!
The Sun is Thy Father!
Thy Mother is the Moon!
The Wind hath borne Thee in its bosom: and Earth hath ever nourished the changeless Godhead of Thy Youth!

Come Thou forth, I say, come Thou forth!
And make all Spirits subject unto Me: So that every Spirit
of the Firmament, and of the Ether, and of the Earth,
and under the Earth, on dry land and in the Water, of
whirling Air and of rushing Fire, and every Spell and
Scourge of God the Vast One, may be obedient unto Me!

CONJURATION OF LUCIFER
(repeat seven times)

LUCIFER: WA-ASARNA TAWA-YAEL
LU, AL-OAI HOOR CHI-FU QADOSH-ASI
AN CHAOS KU-AIWAZ, IAO AIWASS, E!
TA CHI AIWAZ, I-I HADES ASAR-ISA FU,
WA-YA FU IAO PAN, OHE! NOX! CHAOS!
EL QADOSH AIWASS, ASAR-ISA OURDA BES-NI,
O-O ASI EFU-IONILAM Come Lucifer ✠ AMEN ✠

*(The Greeting, Conversation and Invitation, as also the
Conjurations of deputies and subordinates, with their
Greetings, Conversations and Invitations, have been detailed
previously).*

Sub Ritual 656: Of the Sealing of the Pyramid.

*(The Magus with Wand. On the Altar are Incense, Fire, bread,
Wine, the Chain, the Scourge, the Dagger, & the Oil. The bell
is held in the left hand.)*

'Hail, Asi! hail, Hoor Apep! Let
The Silence speech beget!'

(Two strokes on the Bell. Banishing spiral dance.)

'The Words against the Son of Night.
Tahuti speaketh in the Light
Knowledge and Power, twin warriors shake
The Invisible; they roll asunder
The darkness; matter shines, a snake.
Sebek is smitten by the thunder
The Light breaks forth from Under.'

(The Magus goes to the West, in the centre of the base of the Pyramid of Thoth, Asi, and Hoor.)

'O Thou, the Apex of the Plane,
With Ibis head and Phoenix Wand
And Wings of Night! Whose serpents strain
Their bodies, bounding the Beyond.
Thou in the Light & in the Night
Art One, above their moving might!'

The Magus lays the Wand etc. on the altar, and douses their head saying:)

'The Lustral Water! Smite thy flood
Through me lymph, marrow & blood!

(Anointing, say:)

'The Fire Informing! Let the Oil
Balance, assain, assoil!'

The Banishing Spiral Dance

'So Life takes Fire from Death, & runs
Whirling amid the Suns.
Now let my hands unloose the sweet

And shining girdle of Nuit!'

(*Sign of the Enterer:*)

'Homage to Thee, Lord of the Word!'

(*Sign of Silence:*)

'Lord of Silence, Homage to Thee!'

(*Repeat both Signs:*)

'Lord, we adore Thee, still & stirred
Beyond Infinity'

(*The Secret Word.*)

'......'

The Eucharist at the Altar.

'Behold the Perfect One hath said
These are my body's elements
tried & found pure, a golden spoil.'

(*Act accordingly.*)

'Incense and Wine and Fire and Bread
These I consume, true Sacraments,
For the Perfection of the Oil
For I am clothed about with flesh
And I am the Eternal Spirit.
I am the Lord that riseth fresh
From Death, whose glory I inherit

Since I partake with him. I am
The manifestor of the Unseen,
Without me all the land of Khem
Is as if it had not been'

'For from the Silence of the Wand
Unto the Speaking of the Sword.
And back again to the Beyond,
This is the toil & the Reward
This is the Path of HUA – Ho!
This is the path of IAO.'

(Bell.)

'Hail Asi! Hail, thou Wanded Wheel!
Alpha & Delta kissed & came
For Five that feed the Flame.'

(Bell.)

'Hail, Hoor Apep! thou Sword of Steel!
Alpha & Delta and Epsilon
Met in the Shadow of the Pylon
And in Iota did proclaim
That tenfold core & crown of flame.
Hail, Hoor Apep! Unspoken Name!

Hail, Hoor! Hail Asi! Hail Tahuti! Hail,
Asar Un nefer! through the rendered veil.
I am Thyself, with all Thy brilliance decked

Khabs Am Pekht.'

(Thus is the Great Pyramid duly sealed.)

PART III

THE INVOCATION OF HORUS

THE FIRST INVOCATION DISCUSSED HERE INVOLVES SOME SLIGHT departures from those previously examined in parts II and I. Apart from some relatively slight differences of structure, the main distinction is one of type. The mode of use is virtually identical to those preceding it in this book. That is, as a dual natured ritual in which divine invocation is the engine powering the process of spirit conjuring. Many of the procedures involved are therefore the same as those previously discussed. Unlike those that preceded it however, this Invocation is also a rite of 'commemoration', in that the first occasion of its performance marked an important event in the history of the Thelemic tradition.

The ritual of course is the Invocation of Horus, and the occasion it commemorates is the Spring Equinox of 1904, where its performance preceded the reception of *The Book of the Law.*

To introduce this rite then some notes of Crowley's from the period are in order:

INVOCATION OF HORUS ACCORDING TO THE DIVINE VISION OF W., THE SEER.

To be performed before a window open to the E. or N. without incense. The room to be filled with jewels, but only diamonds to be worn. A sword, unconsecrated, 44 pearl beads to be told. Stand. Bright daylight at 12.30 noon. Lock doors.

White robes. Bare feet. Be very loud. Saturday. Use the Sign of Apophis and Typhon.

The above is W.'s answer to various questions posed by P. Preliminary. Banish. L.B.R. Pentagram. L.B.R. Hexagram. Flaming sword. Abrahadabra, Invoke. As

before. (These are P.'s ideas for the ritual. W. replied,
"Omit.")

Of these things omitted two items are in need of
comment: Abrahadabra may refer to some formula derived
from the word, the word itself certainly appears in the
ritual; the Flaming Sword is more certain. This refers to a
technique Crowley derived from the Golden Dawn's 'Shin
of Shin' in the paper called Z2. I analysed this in my essay
The Headless One, to which I respectfully refer the interested
reader (See *Equinox/BJT*. VII. 6).

The rite broke many of what Crowley at that time
considered 'the rules'; there was no banishing, the sword was
unconsecrated and so on. Some of these omissions influence
the form of the Oath with its references to 'unwashen hands'
and so forth. The Magical Ablution normally considered
essential to rites of evocation (see under Invocation of
Typhon-Set) is deliberately omitted in this case. Incidentally,
as this rite comes complete with its own Oath and
Confession, the form employed in the previous examples is
not required.

On the other hand, there are some interesting elements
introduced by Rose Kelly (she is the mysterious W., Crowley
being P.). Note in particular the string of 44 pearl beads,
very suitable for use in Thelemic mantrayoga and devotional
rituals. This string broke after one performance of the rite;
thus, we find reference to sigils drawn with the fingers
(under D in part III), this line is a substitute for an earlier
one mentioning the beads:

My fingers travel on the Beads of Pearl; so run I after
Thee in thy car of glory. By my fingers I invoke Thee!

This is a precedent for other substitutions should they be necessary (for example, references to garments, diamonds and so on). Although such improvisation is permissible and encouraged, I strongly advise that it not extend to the reference to a sword; this weapon is a very important part of the symbolism of *Pyramidos* and the Invocation alike.

The ritual as described here retains most of the strictures imposed by Rose's seer-ship. For example, although the rite employs an Opening and Closing not present in the original, there are no banishing pentagrams etc. In Crowley's performance of the ritual there was a bowl of bull's blood, mentioned in the Oath. This is not strictly required, and may be considered as substituted for by the pearl beads (44 is the number of Daleth Mem 'blood' in Hebrew gematria). Alternatively, the operator can include it, buying a good steak or other bloody beef product and squeezing it into a suitable offering bowl.

Some additional remarks about performance of this ritual are in order. I am unsure how many times I have performed this ritual, but it is certainly upwards of 44 times. Of this I am sure, as I once performed it as a solo ritual every day for 44 days in fulfilment of a vow; this was after Lord Horus 'dropped in' to correct a mistaken opinion of mine some time ago. His presence on this occasion was enough to prostrate me physically, so I recommend the reader to beware dogmatic ideas concerning him or his rites!

On various occasions, I have taken part in the ritual as a group ritual. One such is particularly memorable, taking place some years after the above event. A beautiful image of the god was enshrined in the East, I and another man performed a war dance before it throughout the rite. In the West stood the invoking priest for the occasion; if memory served he borrowed my 44 beads, and 'told them' as he recited the 44 lines of the invocation (those marked by

numbers and letters in the script here). This has certainly
been my practice for many years, and I highly recommend
the reader to acquire some.

Positioned in front of him were all the other participants.
These included two drummers, beating out a rhythm best
expressed as 'dum, dum, dum-de-dum', it also matches the
syllables of the phrase 'watch out, here I come'. Survivors
of the 15th century will recognise this as the beat to which
pikemen advanced in the Italian Wars, chanting a similar
phrase in German. This beat was sustained throughout
the main body of all four parts; stopping only for the short
rhyming sections and the speeches.

The remaining ritualists were in front of the drums,
and everyone joined in the 'strike, strike the master chord...'
chants during the ritual. This performance of the rite was
a phenomenal success, dramatic, impressive and extremely
pleasing to the god, not to mention those taking part. A
couple of days later, the other side of the country, I was
guest at a ritual performed by a certain well-known magical
order. It so happened this was also the Invocation of Horus,
which – to my sensibilities at least – fell flat on its face by
comparison.

THE INVOCATION OF TYPHON-SET

The invocations of Isis and Hecate previously published
were modelled on the 'classic' Tahuti rite. In a similar way,
in addition to the 'classic' Horus Invocation I have included
another invocation modelled upon it. This is the Invocation
of Typhon-Set, to which virtually none of the above remarks
applies. This ritual should not be worked with any but
the NW variant of *Pyramidos*; the Magical Ablutions and
consecrations should in nowise be omitted, these rituals will
not serve to conjure Lucifer but only Belzebuth, and so on.

When the NW variant and either of these invocations are worked together the result is extremely powerful, not to mention dangerous. A great deal of experience with the ritual forms discussed in this book is required before they can be worked safely. Doubtless, this advice will be considered some kind of 'puff', but it is nothing of the kind. The Prince Belzebuth is a 'hot' spirit, and a powerful one. The 'Thelemic Horus' as considered above combines aspects of Set and of Horus. This is not true of Typhon-Set, he is a more ancient form and does not include aspects of Horus. He is chaotic in nature, unforgiving of breaches in ritual decorum, and can seriously disrupt your life if displeased.

THE 'MAGICAL ABLUTION'

This involves drawing a bath, to which add an infusion of the same herbs used in the aspergillus. Recite an 'orison of the bath' as soon as you enter the bath, of which a suitable text follows:

> I have descended, O my darling, into the black shining waters, and I have plucked Thee forth as a black pearl of infinite preciousness.
> I follow Thee, and the waters of Death fight strenuously against me. I pass unto the Waters beyond Death and beyond Life.
> This is the world of the waters of Maim; this is the bitter water that becometh sweet. Thou art beautiful and bitter, O golden one, O my Lord Adonai, O thou Abyss of Sapphire!
> If I say Come up upon the mountains! the celestial waters flow at my word. But thou art the Water beyond the waters.
> Verily and Amen! I passed through the deep sea, and by

the rivers of running water that abound therein, and I
came unto the Land of No Desire.

Yea, also verily Thou art the cool still water of the
wizard fount. I have bathed in Thee, and lost me in Thy
stillness. AMEN.

CLOSING REMARKS

As with the previous installment, I have omitted
such elements as have already appeared. These include
the conversation with spirits and the invitation to share
the sacrament. The Invocation of Horus is unique among
the invocations in that either the conventional Pyramidos
ceremony or the NW variant published here are appropriate
as Opening and Closing rites. Additionally it can be employed
in working with both Lucifer (when the conventional form is
to be employed) and Belzebuth (substituting the NW form).

When the ritual is celebrated at the Spring Equinox,
I strongly recommend that the conventional form be
employed. This is by no means the only time the ritual is
appropriate; it is a very potent rite for a variety of purposes,
useful whenever it is required to raise a lot of magical energy.
This was the way Crowley employed it when contacting
the Secret Chiefs. Incidentally, when a certain moderately
well known occultist asked me what I thought the Secret
Chiefs were, I replied that it is simply a modern term for
old-fashioned spirits. Thus, the ritual is very suitable for the
kind of ceremony discussed here.

The Invocation of Horus

Unprepared and uninvoking Thee, I, ..., am here in Thy Presence – for Thou art Everywhere, O Lord Horus! – to confess humbly before Thee my neglect and scorn of Thee. How shall I humble myself before Thee? Thou art the mighty and unconquered Lord of the Universe: I am a spark of Thine unutterable Radiance. How should I approach Thee? – but Thou art everywhere.

But Thou hast graciously deigned to call me unto Thee, to this exorcism of Art, that I may be Thy servant, Thine Adept, O Bright One, O Sun of Glory! Thou hast called me – should I not hasten to Thy Presence?

With unwashen hands therefore I come unto Thee, and I lament my wandering from Thee – but Thou knowest!

Yea, I have done evil! If one blasphemed Thee, why should I therefore forsake Thee? But Thou art the Avenger; all is with Thee. I bow my neck before Thee; and as once Thy sword was upon it, so I am in Thy hands. Strike if Thou wilt: spare if Thou wilt: but accept me as I am.

My trust is in Thee: shall I be confounded? This Ritual of Art: This Forty and Fourfold Invocation: this Sacrifice of Blood – these I do not comprehend. It is enough if I obey Thy Decree; did Thy Fiat go forth for my eternal misery, were it not my joy to execute Thy Sentence on myself? For why? For that All is in Thee and of Thee; it is enough if I burn up in the intolerable glory of Thy Promise.

Doubtful are the Words: Dark are the Ways: but in Thy Words and Ways is Light. Thus then now as ever, I enter the path of Darkness, if haply so I may attain the Light. Hail!

I

Strike, strike the master chord!
Draw, draw the Flaming Sword!
Crowned Child and Conquering Lord,
Horus, avenger!

O Thou of the Head of the Hawk! Thee, Thee, I invoke!

A. Thou only-begotten-child of Osiris Thy Father, and Isis Thy Mother. He that was slain; She that bore Thee in Her womb, flying from the Terror of the Water. Thee, Thee I invoke!

2. O Thou whose Apron is of flashing white, whiter than the Forehead of the Morning! Thee, Thee, I invoke!

B. O Thou who has Formulated Thy Father and made fertile Thy Mother! Thee, Thee I invoke!

3. O Thou whose garment is of golden glory, with the azure bars of sky! Thee, Thee, I invoke!

C. Thou, who didst avenge the Horror of Death; Thou, the slayer of Typhon! Thou who didst lift Thine arms, and the Dragons of Death were as dust; Thou who didst raise Thine Head, and the Crocodile of the Nile was abased before Thee! Thee, Thee I invoke!

4. O Thou whose Nemyss hideth the Universe with night, the impermeable Blue! Thee, Thee, I invoke!

D. Thou who travellest in the Boat of Ra, abiding at the Helm of the Aftet boat and of the Sektet boat! Thee, Thee, I invoke!

5. Thou who bearest the Wand of Double-Power! Thee, Thee I invoke!

E. Thou about whose presence is shed the darkness of Blue Light, the unfathomable glory of the utmost Ether, the untravelled, the unthinkable immensity of Space. Thou who concentratest all the Thirty Ethers in one darkling sphere of Fire! Thee, Thee I invoke!

6. O Thou who bearest the Rose and Cross of Life and Light! Thee, Thee I invoke!

The Voice of the Five.
The Voice of the Six.
Eleven are the Voices
Abrahadabra!

II

Strike, strike the master chord!
Draw, draw the Flaming Sword!
Crowned Child and Conquering Lord,
Horus, avenger!

1. By thy name of Ra, Hawk of the Sun, the glorious one I invoke Thee!

2. By thy name Harmachis, youth of the Brilliant Morning, I invoke Thee!

3. By thy name, Mau, Lion of the Midday Sun I invoke Thee!

4. By thy name Tum, Hawk of the Even, crimson splendour of the Sunset, I invoke Thee!

5. By thy name Keph-Ra, O Beetle of the hidden Mastery of Midnight, I invoke Thee!

A. By thy name Heru-Pa Kraat, Lord of Silence, beautiful Child that standest on the Dragons of the Deep, I invoke Thee!

B. By thy name of Apollo, O man of Strength and splendour, O poet, O father, I invoke Thee!

C. By thy name of Phoebus, that drivest thy chariot through the heaven of Zeus, I invoke Thee!

D. By thy name of Odin O warrior of the North, O Renown of the Sagas, I invoke Thee!

E. By thy name of Jeheshua, O child of the Flaming Star, I invoke Thee!

F. By Thine own, Thy secret name Hoori, Thee I invoke!

The Names are Five.
The Names are Six.
Eleven are the Names!
Abrahadabra!

Behold! I stand in the midst. Mine is the symbol of Osiris; to Thee are mine eyes ever turned. Unto the splendour of Geburah, the Magnificence of Chesed, the mystery of Daath, thither I lift up mine eyes. This have I sought, and I have sought the Unity: hear Thou me!

III

1. Mine is the Head of the Man, and my insight is keen as the Hawk's. By my Head I invoke Thee!

A. I am the first-begotten child of my Father and Mother. My Father I dead, My Mother bore me with labour and pain and fear. By my body I invoke Thee!

2. About me shine the Diamonds of Radiance white and pure. By their brightness I invoke Thee!

B. Mine is the Red Triangle Reversed, the Sign given of none, save it be of Thee. O Lord! By my Lamen I invoke Thee !

3. Mine is the Garment of white sewn with gold, the flashing abbai that I wear. By my robe I invoke Thee!

C. Mine is the Sign of Apophis and Typhon! By my sign I invoke Thee!

4. Mine is the sphere of white and gold, and mine the blue vigour of the intimate air! By my Crown I invoke Thee!

D. My mystic sigils travel in the bark of the Akasa: so run I after Thee in Thy car of glory. By the spells I invoke Thee!

5. I bear the Wand of Double Power in the Voice of the Master – Abrahadabra! By the word I invoke Thee!

E. Mine are the dark-blue waves of music in the Prophet's song made of old to invoke Thee –

Strike, strike the master chord!
Draw, draw the Flaming Sword!
Crowned Child and Conquering Lord,
Horus, avenger!
By the Song I invoke Thee!

6. In my hand is the Sword of Revenge; let it strike at Thy Bidding! By the Sword I invoke Thee!

The Voice of the Five.
The Voice of the Six.
Eleven are the Voices
Abrahadabra!

IV

Strike, strike the master chord!
Draw, draw the Flaming Sword!
Crowned Child and Conquering Lord,
Horus, avenger!

1. Mine is the of Head of the Hawk! Abrahadabra!

A. I am the only-begotten-child of Osiris my Father, and Isis my Mother. He that was slain; She that bore me in Her womb, flying from the Terror of the Water. Abrahadabra!

2. Mine is the Apron of flashing white, whiter than the Forehead of the Morning! Abrahadabra!

B. I have Formulated My Father and made fertile My Mother! Abrahadabra!

3. Mine is the garment of golden glory, with the azure bars of sky! Abrahadabra!

C. I, who did avenge the Horror of Death; I am, the slayer of Typhon! I who did lift My arms, and the Dragons of Death were as dust; I who did raise My Head, and the Crocodile of the Nile was abased before Me! Abrahadabra!

4. My Nemyss hideth the Universe with night, the impermeable Blue! Abrahadabra!

D. I travel in the Boat of Ra, abiding at the Helm of the Aftet boat and of the Sektet boat! Abrahadabra!

5. I bear the Wand of Double-Power! Abrahadabra!

E. My presence sheds the darkness of Blue Light, the unfathomable glory of the utmost Ether, the untravelled, the unthinkable immensity of Space. I who concentrate all the Thirty Ethers in one darkling sphere of Fire! Abrahadabra!

6. I bear the Rose and Cross of Life and Light! Abrahadabra!

The Voice of the Five.

The Voice of the Six.
Eleven are the Voices
Abrahadabra!

Therefore I say unto Thee: Come Thou forth and dwell in me; so that every Spirit, whether of the Firmament, or of the Ether, upon the Earth or under the Earth, on dry land or in the Water, of Whirling Air or of rushing Fire; and every Spell and Scourge of God the Vast One may be Thee. Abrahadabra!

CONJURATION OF BELZEBUTH

(*repeat seven times*)

CHI PA-SA-GA SU ANKH HORUS CHI NI AUM-HA
LAM
HORUS BES, EL IOAL BES HORUS QADOSH BALAE
ASI
SU EL WA KA LE SU ASAR KU SA
ANKH IOAL AHAH OAZ IOAL ANKH TA AKABA GA
HORUS BES, EL IOAL BES HORUS QADOSH BALAE
ASI
CHI PA-SA-GA SU ANKH HORUS CHI NI AUM-HA
LAM
NI QADOSH ASAR TA QADOSH NI ABRA PAN AB
AUM-HA ASI SA GA ASI LAM AB ANKH OA:
Come, BELZEBUTH, ✠ AMEN ✠

(*The Greeting, Conversation and Invitation, as also the Conjurations of deputies and subordinates, with their Greetings, Conversations and Invitations, have been detailed previously*).

AN INVOCATION OF TYPHON-SET

I

1. O Thou God with the Head of the Typhonian Beast! Thee, Thee, I invoke!

2. O Thou God of Destruction and Desolation! Thee, Thee I invoke!

3. O Thou who didst slay Osiris, and whose wrath even Isis doth flee! Thee, Thee I invoke!

4. O Thou who hateth a household well established! Thee, Thee I invoke!

5. O Thou Terrible and Invisible God, the God with an Empty Spirit! Thee, Thee, I invoke!

6. O Thou, who dost make clear the Path of Ra; Thou, the slayer of Apep! Thee, Thee I invoke!

7. O Thou rebel against the gods who remains unconquered! Thee, Thee, I invoke!

8. O Thou who travellest in the Boat of Ra, abiding at the Prow of the Aftet boat and of the Sektet boat! Thee, Thee, I invoke!

9. O Thou who dost bear the might and the power of God! Thee, Thee I invoke!

10. O Thou Primeval God, Lord of the Seven Stars of the Northern Heaven! Thee, Thee I invoke!

11. O Thou who dwelleth in the Invisible Darkness! Thee, Thee I invoke!

12. O Thou that standeth in the Lake of Fire! Thee, Thee I invoke!

13. O Thou who bearest the Sword of Revenge! Thee, Thee I invoke!

II

I invoke Thee, Typhon-Set, I perform thy ceremonies of divination, for I invoke Thee by thy powerful name in words which thou canst not refuse to hear:

IO ERBETH, IO PAKERBETH, IO BOLKHOSETH, IO PATATHNOX, IO SORO, IO NEBOUTOSOUALETH, AKTIOPHI, ERESHKIGAL, NEBOPOSOALETH, ABERAMENTHOOU, LERTHEXANAX, ETHRELUOTH, NEMAREBA, AEMINA.

1. By thy name of Typhon, Dragon of Storm, the powerful one, Thee, Thee I invoke!

2. By thy name Reshef, Lord of plague and pestilence, Thee, Thee I invoke!

3. By thy name of Aeshma Daeva, that ever turnest about the Pole, Thee, Thee I invoke!

4. By thy name Sebek, Lord of the Glittering Star, Thee, Thee I invoke!

5. By thy name of Mentu, Warrior God of the Sun, Thee, Thee I invoke!

6. By thy name Baal Sabaoth, Lord of the Seven, Thee, Thee I invoke!

7. By thy name of Loki, trickster and magician of the Sagas, Thee, Thee I invoke!

8. By thy name Ganesh, the God who breakest down obstruction, Thee, Thee I invoke!

9. By thy name of Ahrimanes, Lord of Darkness, Thee, Thee I invoke!

10. By thy name Exu, Lord of the Crossroads, Thee, Thee I invoke!

11. By Thy name of Nubti, the Golden God, Thee, Thee I invoke!

12. By Thy name Achilles, sire-surpassing storm of battle, Thee, Thee I invoke!

13. By Thy name of Set, the slayer of Osiris, Thee, Thee I invoke!

14. By Thine own, Thy secret name, ABERA-MENTHOU, Thee, Thee I invoke!

III

1. Thou art He, The Lord of the Wilderness, by the Wilderness I invoke Thee!

2. Typhon! Nubti-Set! Aberamenthou! By whatsoever names I call thee, thou art Thyself, nameless unto eternity! Thee, Thee I invoke!

3. Thou art He the Terrible and Invisible God, that dwellest in the empty wind! By the Void I invoke Thee!

4. Thine are the Seventy-Two conspirators against Osiris! Thee, Thee I invoke!

5. Thou art He, the Headless Spirit, having Sight in the feet! By thy Sight I invoke Thee!

6. Thine is the Sign of Apophis and Typhon! Thee, Thee I invoke!

7. Thou art He, whose mouth ever flameth! By the Flame I invoke Thee!

8. Thou whose Name causeth the stars, seas, earth and underworld to tremble! Thee, Thee I invoke!

9. Thou art He that lighteneth and thundereth! By the Storm I invoke Thee!

10. Thou art the Avenger judged innocent by the gods! Thee, Thee I invoke!

11. Thou art He, whose bones are of Iron! By thy metal I invoke Thee!

12. Thou that art seated upon the Gates of the Underworld! Thee, Thee I invoke!

13. In Thy hand is the Sword of Death, that striketh the traitors! By the Sword I invoke Thee!

IV

1. Mine is the Head of the Beast of Typhon! Abera-Menthou!

2. I am a God of Destruction and Desolation. Abera-Menthou!

3. I am the slayer of Osiris, whose wrath even Isis doth flee. Abera-Menthou!

4. It is I that hateth a household well established! Abera-Menthou!

5. I am the Terrible and Invisible God, the God with an Empty Spirit! Abera-Menthou!

6. I make clear the Path of Ra; for I am the slayer of Apep! Abera-Menthou!

7. I am the rebel against the gods who remains unconquered! Abera-Menthou!

8. I travel in the Boat of Ra, abiding at the Prow of the Aftet boat and of the Sektet boat! Abera-Menthou!

9. I bear the might and the power of God! Abera-Menthou!

10. I am the Primeval God, Lord of the Seven Stars of the Northern Heaven! Abera-Menthou!

11. I am he who dwelleth in the Invisible Darkness! Abera-Menthou!

12. I am he that standeth in the Lake of Fire! Abera-Menthou!

13. I am the God who beareth the Sword of Death! Abera-Menthou!

14. It is by my hand the magician doth mount unto heaven! Abera-Menthou!

Therefore I say unto Thee: Come Thou forth and dwell in me; so that every Spirit, whether of the Firmament, or of the Ether, upon the Earth or under the Earth, on dry land or in the Water, of Whirling Air or of rushing Fire; and every Spell and Scourge of God the Vast One may be Thee. Abera-Menthou!

THE RITUAL OF THE PYRAMID:
NORTH WEST VARIANT

The Building of the Pyramid. (Sub ritual 672)

*(The Magus with Sword. On the altar are oil and water. In his
left hand the Bell he taketh.)*

'Hail, Asi! Hail, Tahuti! Let
The Silence speech beget!'

(Two strokes on the Bell. Banishing spiral dance.)

'The deeds that bring the Sun to Light
Set-Hoor performeth in the Night
Force and Fire, thy progress make
Through Night to bright day's wonder:
From flood Khem doth awake.
Apep is smitten by the thunder
The Light breaks forth from Under!'

*(He goes to the place halfway between Asi in the SW and
Tahuti in the E, and faces the NW, place of Hoor-Apep.)*

'Thou North-West Angle of the Plane,
With Asses head and Sword of Steel
Girt with a Snake - to flood again -
That all of Khem Thy waters feel;
O Thou red ruler of the Night
Bring lustful power and furious might!'
(Alt: Bring dire revenge and furious might!)

(He lays down the Sword etc. and douses his head)

'The Lustral Water! Smite thy flood
Through me lymph, marrow & blood!'

(*Anointing the Brow, say:*)

'The Fire Informing! Let the Oil
Balance, assain, assoil!'

The Invoking Spiral Dance (with sword)

'The Logos is a sword, & runs
Whirling amid the Suns.

Hail Thoth! Pace the Path, and make
Thy rounds of the circled snake!'

(*Sign of Set Fighting:*)

'Homage to Thee, Lord of Force!'

(*Sign of Apophis and Typhon:*)

'Lord of Fire, Homage to Thee!'

(*Repeat both Signs:*)

'Lord, we adore Thee, still & stirred
 Beyond Infinity.'

(*The Secret Word.*)

'............'

'For from the Speaking of the Sword

To the fulfilling of the Wheel

And back again to the glad word,

And to the sacramental meal

This is the Path of HUA   Ho!

This is the path of IAO.'

(Bell.)

'Hail Thoth! Above the Serpents Strife!

Alpha & Delta kissed & came

For Five that feed the Flame.'

(Bell.)

'Hail, Asi! thou Wheel of Life!

Alpha & Delta and Epsilon

Met in the Shadow of the Pylon

And in Iota did proclaim

That tenfold core & crown of flame.

Hail, Hoor-Apep! Unspoken Name!'

(Thus is the Great Pyramid duly builded.)

The Sealing of the Pyramid.

(The Magus with Sword. On the Altar are Water and Oil, in his left hand the Bell he taketh.)

'Hail, Asi! Hail, Tahuti! Let
The Silence speech beget!'

(Two strokes on the Bell. Banishing spiral dance.)

'The deeds that bring the Sun to Light
Set-Hoor performeth in the Night
Force and Fire, thy progress make
Through Night to bright day's wonder:
From flood Khem doth awake.
Apep is smitten by the thunder
The Light breaks forth from Under!'

(He goes to the place halfway between Asi in the SW and Tahuti in the E, and faces the NW, place of Hoor-Apep.)

'Thou North-West Angle of the Plane,
With Asses head and Sword of Steel
Girt with a Snake – to flood again –
That all of Khem Thy waters feel;
O Thou red ruler of the Night
Bring lustful power and furious might!'
(Alt: Bring dire revenge and furious might!)

(He lays down the Sword etc. and douses his head)

'The Lustral Water! Smite thy flood
Through me lymph, marrow & blood!'

(Anointing the Brow, say:)

'The Fire Informing! Let the Oil
Balance, assain, assoil!'

'The Logos is a sword, & runs
Whirling amid the Suns.
Hail Thoth! Pace the Path, and break
The bounds of the circled snake!'

(Sign of Set Fighting:)

'Homage to Thee, Lord of Force!'

(Sign of Apophis and Typhon:)

'Lord of Fire, Homage to Thee!'

(Repeat both Signs:)

'Lord, we adore Thee, still & stirred
 Beyond Infinity.'
(The Secret Word.)

'............'

The Eucharist at the Altar.

'Behold the Perfect One hath said
These are my body's elements
tried & found pure, a golden spoil.

(Act accordingly.)

'Incense and Wine and Fire and Bread
These I consume, true Sacraments,
For the Perfection of the Oil
For I am clothed about with flesh
And I am the Eternal Spirit.
I am the Lord that riseth fresh
From Death, whose glory I inherit
Since I partake with him. I am
The manifestor of the Unseen,
Without me all the land of Khem
Is as if it had not been'

'For from the Speaking of the Sword
To the fulfilling of the Wheel
And back again to the glad word,
And to the sacramental meal
This is the Path of HUA   Ho!
This is the path of IAO.'

(Bell.)

'Hail Thoth! Above the Serpents Strife!
Alpha & Delta kissed & came
For Five that feed the Flame.'

(Bell.)

'Hail, Asi! thou Wheel of Life!
Alpha & Delta and Epsilon
Met in the Shadow of the Pylon
And in Iota did proclaim
That tenfold core & crown of flame.
Hail, Isis, She who knows the Name!'

Hail, Hoor! Hail Asi! Hail Tahuti! Hail,

Asar Un nefer! through the rendered veil.

I am Thyself, with all Thy brilliance decked

Khabs Am Pekht.'

(Thus is the Great Pyramid duly sealed.)

www.ingramcontent.com/pod-product-compliance
Lightning Source LLC
LaVergne TN
LVHW021409080426
835508LV00020B/2521